THE PROBABLE WORLD

THE
PROBABLE
WORLD

Lawrence Raab

Penguin Poets

PENGUIN BOOKS

Published by the Penguin Group
Penguin Putnam Inc., 375 Hudson Street,
New York, New York 10014, U.S.A.
Penguin Books Ltd, 27 Wrights Lane,
London W8 5TZ, England
Penguin Books Australia Ltd, Ringwood,
Victoria, Australia
Penguin Books Canada Ltd, 10 Alcorn Avenue,
Toronto, Ontario, Canada M4V 3B2
Penguin Books (N.Z.) Ltd, 182–190 Wairau Road,
Auckland 10, New Zealand

Penguin Books Ltd, Registered Offices:
Harmondsworth, Middlesex, England

First Published in Penguin Books 2000

1 3 5 7 9 10 8 6 4 2

LIBRARY OF CONGRESS CATALOGING-IN-PUBLICATION DATA
Raab, Lawrence, 1946–
    The probable world / Lawrence Raab.
      p.   cm.
    ISBN 0 14 05.8921 X
    I. Title.
    PS3568.A2 P76 2000
    813'.54—dc21   99–055293

Printed in the United States of America
Set in Bembo
Designed by Jennifer Ann Daddio

For Stephen Dunn

ACKNOWLEDGMENTS

Antaeus, "All Day"

Crab Orchard Review, "The Invisible," "Fragile"

The Denver Quarterly, "Probable Facts"

The Gettysburg Review, "Meaningful Things," "Hunters," "Love,"
   "False Nocturne," "My Spiritual Life"

Great River Review, "High School Days," "Three Exercises"

The Journal, "Why the Truth Is Hidden"

The Kenyon Review, "A Small Lie"

Lungfish Review, "The Cremation of Shelley"

The New England Review, "Figuring It Out," "Years Later," "Envy,"
   "The Best Days," "The Band Was Still Playing"

The New Republic, "Respect," "Hamlet's Problems," "My Life at the
   Movies"

The New Yorker, " 'My Soul Is a Light Housekeeper,' " "The Revised
   Versions"

The Paris Review, "The Luminists"

Poetry, "The Lost Things"

Prairie Schooner, "Why Tragedy Is the Wrong Word," "Bad Music"

River City, "Dreaming of the Afterlife"

River Styx, "Another Argument About the Impossible"

Salmagundi, "My Life Before I Knew It"

Virginia Quarterly Review, "The Questions Poems Ask," "Permanence,"
   "Big Ideas," "The Night Sky"

I would like to thank Yaddo, the MacDowell Colony, and Williams
College for their generous support.

*A fellow will remember a lot of things you wouldn't think
he'd remember. You take me. One day, back in 1896, I was
crossing over to Jersey on the ferry, and as we pulled out,
there was another ferry pulling in, and on it there was a girl
waiting to get off. A white dress she had on. She was
carrying a white parasol. I only saw her for one second. She
didn't see me at all, but I bet a month hasn't gone by since,
that I haven't thought of that girl.*

—BERNSTEIN TO THOMPSON
IN *CITIZEN KANE*

*Then there is a time in life
when you just take a walk:
and you walk in your own landscape.*
—WILLEM DE KOONING

CONTENTS

3

4

1

WHY THE TRUTH IS HIDDEN

First, I'd like to thank God,
said the pilot,
shot down and rescued. Later

after the big game the best player
says it again, and the announcer
nods. It's right

for the winners to be grateful,
and useful for their thanks
to sound like modesty, since America

doesn't like a man who's good
at what he does and wants
to talk about it.

And the losers? They know
His ways are dark, His path
difficult. They understand justice

isn't always what it seems,
or else they couldn't, who've lost
the most, bear it. Surely

God was wise not to speak
to us anymore. After all,
what did that accomplish?

Endless arguments
about who knows who's right.
Centuries of murder.

Every religion, Pascal said,
that does not affirm that God
is hidden is not true.

That's what, in His disappointment,
He must have decided. Stay back,
keep quiet, let them come to you.

LOVE

In a sudden rage a man kills his wife.
Then he drives back to his house.
There's no getting away from this, he thinks.
He hadn't tried to hide anything.
The police will show up soon.
He has a gun, so he tells himself
he should do it now, outside on the lawn.
Or he could get back in the car,
drive around for a while. It's hard to decide.
His dog is out there, certain
something is wrong. No,
he's not going to shoot the dog.
His heart's already broken,
knowing he's killed his wife
whom he still believes he loved, knowing now
he's a man who could do that kind of thing.
The dog comes over to him.
He thinks the dog wants to help
and it breaks his heart again
to feel he'd been kinder
to his dog than his wife, or at least
kind enough to deserve this trust,
this affection. Love? he thinks.
Would that be going too far?
He walks inside, sits down,
puts the gun in his mouth.
But the dog scratches at the door,
keeps on scratching until
he gets up, lets her in, half-aware
he's made a choice.
How can he kill himself in front of his dog?
He strokes her head.
Good girl, he says, and then

other things no one says to a dog.
If only she would go to another room.
But she won't leave, and no matter what
he tells her, she refuses to be comforted.

RESPECT

A latticework of trees at dusk, silhouettes
of sky shading upwards into the darkest blue.
I'm thinking of Frost stepping out of his cabin
to watch the snow falling, evening coming down.
I've seen the place, walked around the chair
he wrote in, felt a suitable respect.
I've seen the film his publishers made
where he wanders off to chop some wood
as if that was what he always did
before beginning a poem. When in fact . . .
But why should we care about that?
So what if he was a terrible man. So what
if Philip Larkin hated everybody, and wrote
his friends to say how much
he hated his other friends, and finally
all the world except, perhaps, the Queen.
He knew how to keep it from his work.
I'd like to believe he found a place that mattered
among those words, but what do I know?
For him it may have mattered less and less.
What's to be done with all the rubbish
of a life when you know so little
can be made memorable? They got famous
and mean. They were rude at parties
and lost their friends, or couldn't be sure
if they had or not. They got old
and were afraid. Now I'm imagining
Frost opening the door to see
snow coming down fast into that field,
and thinking of nothing new to say.
But by then the world should look
the way you've written it.
So what if the world changes. So what
if you suspect, late at night when you can't

drink yourself any closer to sleep,
that all your bitterness adds up to nothing
but more bitterness, and those few books
are what you used to be.
So what if that's sad, and it is. So what
if there's no other way to end.

AMERICAN LIGHT

In those days a traveler prepared himself
to be astonished. There were wonders
in every direction—the mountains *stupendous,*
the precipices *lofty,* the waters
profoundly deep. No one settled for anything
less than the sublime. Don't fool yourself.
You also would have cherished the Idea
of Nature, how inside it a better self
lives to repair whatever might befall you—
any calamity, any disgrace.
This is the world without encumbrance,
that famous light trembling across it.
Consider the hush of the storm on the far horizon,
that abandoned boat by the shore. And further west—
woods *of the dimmest shade,* the solitude
utter and unbroken. Now you've climbed
some great cliff. You're feeling
like a new man, overwhelmed
by everything you can see, certain
this world will never fail you.

A SMALL LIE

I

The reporter expected the place would be
"sinister beyond words," and it wasn't.
It seemed "harmless." The barracks
were painted "a pleasant soft green."

So many rooms, emptied of their cries,
turn into dingy schools,
the bunkhouses of a summer camp . . .

Decades later, the guard they captured
was a frail old man, who claimed
he'd been somewhere else, working at a desk.
When the survivors recognized him,
he said they'd made a terrible mistake.

"Do you know what this is?"
the mugger asked my friend, showing him a gun,
and after he'd taken his money
he said, "You know, I wasn't going to hurt you."

Many had been told
they were just going off to work.
How could they have believed it?

2

But now we think we've learned
something about evil—how it likes to appear
ordinary, like anybody's grandfather.

Sometimes the kid next door
buys a rifle and kills his family.
The neighbors are shocked,
then admit he'd always been quiet
and a little strange. Now they can see it,
how he wasn't like the others,
their own sons and daughters.

"I saw him coming," my friend was saying,
"and I should have turned away.
But I kept walking."

And as he walked he told himself a small lie—
Of course this isn't going to happen
—which was what he'd told himself
many times before, when it had been the truth.

DREAMING OF THE AFTERLIFE

When I saw my father I was looking
through the windows of my sixth-grade classroom.

Out where the playground would have been
my father was walking with a friend
I didn't recognize, though I understood
(as we understand such things in dreams)

he was a friend, and both of them were dead.
I knew I wasn't being summoned,
but I went outside, and my father stopped.
He said he'd planned to visit me the next day.

There were many people he wanted to see.
And then he told me I had done
a good job. Meaning the funeral, I thought,
all the arrangements. I could tell

he hadn't found the right words
and now he wouldn't, since I'd appeared like this.
And I remember how his friend stepped back
when my father spoke, and turned away

to allow us our privacy, even if
that wasn't really necessary.

ALL DAY

Others cannot escape their subjects.
History, injustice, whole countries
gone begging for a song. For them: the silence
of high places, the risks of an open field,
and that shattering light in which
a man might find a way
beyond himself, each new burden becoming
another piece of luck.
                Who can be content
with the sadness of the past? Here:
the bright swerve and rise
of a small fire, the smell
of woodsmoke—I knew what I'd be reminded of,
how many rooms and nights would appear,
how the word *sadness* would have to be
resisted.
        Just beyond
this house with its curling tendril of smoke
there's a meadow in which deer gather,
eating their way through the afternoon.
When a dog barks they look up,
wait, and return. Birds
continue to sing.
           Somewhere
heroic deeds have already been performed,
significant acts of betrayal.
In the squares of besieged cities
the wounded are still crying out.
Some ask for help, but others
beg their friends to stay away, the shells
keep falling, and truly
nothing can be done.
             So all day
passes, until at evening

the field seems empty, the dog
is asleep, the fire is ash,
soft and delicate. You might
even kneel down and touch it.

THE LOST THINGS

In the attic or cellar, back in some drawer, way back
on the top shelf of somebody's closet
were the stamp albums and the baseball cards,
both cap pistols in their leather holsters.
In our house nothing was actually lost,
even if we didn't know where to look.

So those guns rusted, and the pages of books
turned brown. No one had taken proper care,
but that wasn't the point. Permanence
was never the point. Instead:
the desire not to feel regret.
When the time came,

the house up for sale, every closet
open to inspection, I took what I thought
I wanted, even if not to decide
was what I wanted, to leave things
in their places, let the pictures crack and the mice
chew at the spines of the Hardy Boys and

Tom Swift and His Submarine,
Tom Swift and His Rocket Ship,
Tom Swift in the Caves of Nuclear Fire.
Not selling them or throwing them away,
not saving them either. The way we think
anything can be remembered, if memory
is like opening the right drawer
or taking a box down from a high shelf
for no particular reason.

THE CREMATION OF SHELLEY

August 15, 1822

All around was scenery—
the ocean and its islands, watchtowers
along the coast, mountains
glittering like marble. Trelawny imagined
the spirit of his friend soaring above him.

And he thought, We're no better
than a pack of dogs
dragging him back into the light.
Three white wands
marked the place where he'd been buried,

lime thrown over him, the yellow sand
shovelled in. And now
they had to dig him out. Who could speak?
Even Byron was silent.
When they heard the hollow sound

of iron on bone, Byron asked
if Trelawny would save the skull for him,
but remembering that he had formerly
used one as a drinking-cup, I was determined
Shelley's should not be so profaned.

After the fire was lit they poured
wine over the body, causing the flames
to glisten and quiver. Then the corpse
fell open, and the heart
was laid bare. Byron turned away,

walked back to the beach,
swam out to his boat. Leigh Hunt
stayed inside his carriage. Everything

turned to ash, *but what surprised us all*
was that the heart remained entire.

The poet's heart! Of course
it should resist the fire.
But why? As fitting that it burn,
if brighter than the rest.
Trelawny reached in and snatched it out.

No one saw him do it,
though his hand was badly hurt.
Every detail, he would write,
of the life of a man of genius
is interesting. But no more

about the heart—how much
he wanted it. *I collected*
the human ashes and placed them in a box.
Buried in Rome
with the appropriate ceremonies.

THE BAND WAS STILL PLAYING

> From aft came the tunes of the band. It was
> a ragtime tune. I don't know what. Then
> there was "Autumn" . . . The ship was
> turning gradually on her nose . . . The band
> was still playing. I guess all of them went
> down.
>
> —Harold Bride, wireless operator
> on the *Titanic*

I just want to imagine them playing,
the touch that makes disaster beautiful,
like the ship with her lights still on.
We can all admire
the man with strength enough
to give his place to the woman and her child.
But who decided they'd continue?
Or was it understood
this was better than fighting
for a boat, or drinking at the bar?
Perhaps only a few of them stayed behind.
But I want the whole band to be there,
and I want them to feel certain
they've never played this well before.
Someone says, "Let's do 'Autumn' again."
Or no one has to say it, since now
they are leaderless and complete
and what carries them from measure to measure
is a kind of joy
I want to believe
no one near me will ever feel.

WHY TRAGEDY IS THE WRONG WORD

It's too grand for the worst
that happens to most of us.
We suffer heartaches, die in disasters.
Think of the truck out of control
on the thruway, or the bridge
about to collapse. Think of the terrorist
planting his bomb.

Not one of us
is spared such imaginings.
Touching down, the plane explodes.
A few survive; hundreds
are scattered across a cornfield.
Then *disaster* sounds insufficient, even cruel.

Then it seems right to forget
the old definitions: how tragedy required
stature and knowledge,
how it depended on a hidden weakness,
an inevitable fall, how it made
death look noble and necessary.

YEARS LATER

Sometimes my father returns
in a dream, backlit
in a room that belongs
to none of our houses. Although
we do not speak, I know
he hasn't died. That was
a mistake, my error. And always
I'm grateful to understand this.

★

Now I can start over.
Now I can begin imagining you.
In those beautiful black-and-white photographs
you're young and handsome, posing
beside some monument, or proudly
holding up a string of fish.
Here is the lake in New Hampshire,
early morning with the mist in place.
Here's your rusty green tackle box
and that old wooden rowboat.
You slide it into the water, adjust the oars.
When you reach the place
in the cove among the waterlilies,
you cast into the fog, watch it rising
around you until all the cottages
emerge in bright duplicates,
still guarding their sleepers.
Then the first breeze begins
rearranging those reflections, and your boat,
unanchored, drifts through them.
You open the thermos of coffee.
It's Saturday. This is happiness, you think.

★

If we could never speak to each other
whose fault was that? In every family
someone is more silent, and the conversation
circles around him, the jokes
turn against him, which he permits.
I always thought you knew
what you wanted your life to be.
And when you got it, you couldn't
imagine anything else you might need,
anything you should have needed.
Or you kept it to yourself.

★

It's Saturday, and you
haven't caught a single fish,
but that doesn't matter.
You give yourself another hour.
Even then it won't really matter.
Your wife is still asleep. Perhaps
I'm back there also, still asleep.
But no—this should be earlier.
Now you can see the cornfields
behind the cottage. You can hear the crows.
A screen door opens, and she steps out
onto the porch in her bathrobe.
She waves, but not to call you in.
Everything looks so clear.
I should let you go.

★

In another dream
soon after my father's death,
I found myself walking through a town
I'd never known, down a worn cobbled street,

and I saw him in the back of a wooden cart.
We noticed each other without astonishment.
How are you? I asked. Meaning:
How does it feel to be dead?
I'm fine, he answered quietly.
But I could see this was awkward for him,
and I thought perhaps he wasn't
permitted to speak of his new life.
He was almost gone when I asked,
And is she there with you?
How is she? Fine, he replied.
She's fine too. How strange, I thought
as I began to wake—
that he would say so little, that I
could give him so little to say.

2

ANOTHER ARGUMENT ABOUT
THE IMPOSSIBLE

Even if we agree in principle that a poem can be
about anything, you still want to claim
it cannot include space aliens,
since by their very nature (you insist)
they are silly. And even if belief
is a subject that's stood the test of time,
a poem about a man who believes in space aliens
will be a poem about a man who is either
silly or demented. Belief requires
a world of consequence all around it:
men, women, nature, history, and so on.
Reality, of course, is another matter, but see
what happens (you continue) when these
are put together, as in: "My work
concerns the nature of reality, belief,
and space aliens." It would be different
if we knew they were there, but we don't,
and a poem cannot afford to adopt
such a wait-and-see attitude toward the world
which, after all, has provided so many
more compelling subjects. No (you conclude),
not even a poem that argues against them
can survive their presence,
not even if the aliens never appear,
never do or say anything, never threaten us
with their neutron blasters, never steal our women
to populate their planet, not even if their ships
remain hidden, and we are never taken up in them
to be probed and instructed, dazzled and released.

IN THE GARDEN

Before the Fall
Adam and Eve tended the garden,
pruning and ordering,
and when they slept
the lavish trees and shrubs grew
just enough to require attention.

They didn't call it work.
It was what they did,
being part of a plan
they couldn't see the shape of.
But they must have felt
how pleased God was to observe them.
One day was what they had, the same day,

in which they worked separately.
At night did they dream? I think
they could not have dreamt,
since the past was the same
as the future—neither hope
nor despair, only tendrils

and branches, the heaviness
of flowers leaning over the path
that led from the man to the woman
and which, each day, needed to be cleared.

"MY SOUL IS A LIGHT HOUSEKEEPER"

Error in the printing of the line
"My soul is a lighthouse keeper,"
by an unknown female poet

Bored with the high drama of watching,
I see myself bound always to your absence,
sending out my pure circle of light so you
will know where I am, and how close
you might come to disaster. Imagine, love,
the tedium of this watch. On almost every day
nothing happens. And isn't it wrong to yearn
for a great storm just to feel important?
I'll let you go, then. Why shouldn't my house
be my own, and my soul its keeper?
This work I needn't take so seriously
since I've learned what pleases me, the light
of late afternoon through that window,
the intricate cobwebs I won't disturb.
I know you don't want to think of me
not always thinking of you, brave and imperiled.
I'm sure you'll write to say: *How can you change*
so completely? You're not the woman
I thought I knew. And I'm not,
but understand, dear, it wasn't such a great change.
Imagine you could have seen that side of me
at the beginning, when we walked
for hours along the shore, and you were so certain
I was yours just because you loved me.

THE REVISED VERSIONS

Even Samuel Johnson found that ending
unbearable, and for over a hundred years
Lear was allowed to live, along with Cordelia,
who marries Edgar, who tried so hard
to do the right thing. It's not easy
being a king, having to worry every day

about the ambitions of your friends.
Who needs a bigger castle?
Let's sleep on it, Macbeth might tell his wife,
wait and see what comes along.
So Antony keeps his temper, takes Cleopatra
aside to say: We need to talk this through.

And Hamlet? Send him back to school to learn
no one ever really pleases his father.
And while he's reading he'll remember
how pretty Ophelia was, how much
she admired his poems.
Why not make what you can of love?

It's what we want for ourselves,
wary of starting a fight, anxious
to avoid another scene, having suffered
through too many funerals and heard
how eloquently the dead are praised
who threw their lives away.

GREAT ART

There's so much I don't want to look at,
big religious scenes especially,
big historical battles,
almost anything, in fact, containing
large numbers of people.

Three or four people—that's the right number
for a painting. Then you can think
about what they might mean to each other,
why they're standing around that beach
at sunset, walking toward that mountain.

Or they're at home: a woman sewing, a child
playing, a dog, a man at the door,
much more ominous, I'm sure, than the artist
intended. And I like that, imagining
this isn't what I was supposed to feel,

the way I'm pleased with small imperfections,
stains and wrinkles, erasures particularly,
where you sense the artist changing his mind.
And sometimes a shape's been painted over,
although the ghost of it remains.

In Vermeer's *Girl Asleep at a Table*
she leans on one hand, dreaming
perhaps of love. Behind her there's a mirror
in which nothing is reflected. Once,
x-rays have shown, this was a portrait of a man.

And we would have understood, given
the conventions of the time, he was the subject

of her thoughts. Why take him away?
It's better, I want Vermeer
to have decided, not to show that much.

Let her keep her dream to herself.
Let the light be our secret.

BAD MUSIC

My friend left the concert even before
the first piece was over, insisting
it simply hadn't done what music had to do—
there was no life to it, no human feeling,
no way you could be moved. I said
he hadn't understood, that all
the possible pleasures of those sounds
were lost on him, on both of us, and so
we couldn't make a judgment. You just can't say
it was *bad*. Yes I can, he said.

At the end of *The Metamorphosis*
Gregor crawls out of his room to hear his sister
playing the violin. *Was he an animal,*
that music had such an effect on him?
No one is really listening.
And yet Gregor's sister was playing so beautifully.
Remember, I tell my students, Gregor never
liked music before. Why is he drawn to it now?
Why does he feel the presence
of that unknown nourishment he always craved?

My students are asking, But why
did he turn into a bug in the first place?
It's a hot April afternoon, and no one
really cares why he turned into a bug.
Outside, music is playing much too loudly,
frisbees are being tossed back and forth
by those freed from worrying about such questions,
and I can see them moving in time
to that heavy insistent beat, across the green lawns,
feeling exactly what they want to feel.

DOGS

I never liked the idea.
Didn't animals belong outside?
Wasn't it wrong to make them
feel like people, talking to them
as if they understood?

Of course they understood
some of the time, I said,
but anything small enough gets scared
when you raise your voice.
A well-trained dog, we read

when we got the dog, is a happy dog.
Your dog, I told my wife.
And yours, I told my daughter.
But all the better arguments
were on their side: loyalty,

companionship, and every time
we came home the dog welcomed us,
so of course we started
talking to her. Then sometimes
I said I'd take her out.

I said I wanted to smoke a cigarette
and I did, even though
I liked the way she waited by the door
when I called her name,
the way it was so easy to make her happy.

FRIENDSHIP

No confessions exactly. But knowing how much
to disclose. When it's appropriate. And never
as a test. I suppose there are

passionate friendships, marked
by quarrels, recriminations, tearful forgiveness.
But that sounds too much like love,

and I want to reserve for friendship
the obligation of listening to those quarrels,
slanders not always meant, sometimes justified.

The friend's duty is to take sides,
and sometimes not to. We've heard so much
about telling the truth

about our feelings. Who loves us then?
Maybe a mother or a father, someone unable
to avoid responsibility. When Thoreau said,

"I never met a worse man than myself,"
he didn't want the world to listen
to every piece of evidence. He had

what we all need, a sense of tact.
As the good friend says, "Tell me about it."
Or decides it's proper not to speak.

PROBABLE FACTS

You wouldn't believe my poem.
So I told you it was the truth.
Doesn't matter, you replied,
citing a certain detail. It isn't probable.
What's probable is boring, everyday stuff.
I like everyday stuff, you said.
The truth is more interesting,
I insisted. Facts are more interesting.
Some facts, you said. Probable facts.
Then what if I change "repeatedly" to "twice"?
Better, you conceded, and then
try changing "up north" to "backyard,"
and maybe "history" to "argument."
What's wrong with "history"? How can "history"
possibly be untrue? It's too big,
you said, for this moment. And at the end
instead of "setting your house on fire,"
I'd prefer "tearing up your letter."
But that's completely different!
Yes, you said, but it sounds like the truth.

HUNTERS

This last cold winter killed the flame bush
at the edge of our meadow, although I'm sure
those hungry deer helped it along.
They should have eaten less.
Next year if the snow's as deep
they'll have nothing. But they're all
so tame and stupid they stand around that field
in the middle of hunting season, as if they trusted
the signs that say Keep Out. A farmer
in Vermont used to paint COW on the sides
of his cows and they still got shot.
And I've heard that serious hunters
dress in camouflage, figuring that even a red vest
could be some drunkard's idea of a deer.
Somebody's out there in the cold with a gun
thinking, Man and Nature, Mortal Combat,
and then a flick of white—
how could he tell it was laundry?
Or his friend unwrapping a sandwich?
It's the price we pay for woods nearby.
I'm not complaining. So many others
have it much worse all the time. Step out
on the street at the wrong moment
and it's over. You were in their line of fire,
or you looked like somebody who'd just
burned them on a drug deal.
Or maybe they were driving by and since
you were nobody one of them said,
"Let's blow that guy away." It was bad luck,
though if they'd known you, and if
they'd needed one, they would have found a reason.

THE FIRST LIE

Completely transparent.
It wasn't my idea. The same lie
children turn to. *She made me do it.*
Picking up the broken pieces
each parent must decide
how far to press the matter,
whether to make a lesson of it, or seeing
the child begin to tremble, to stop
this side of tears. God, of course,

knew those two were as good as children,
which was what He'd had in mind:
to watch them in the garden,
to keep them safe, so they
would thank Him. And yet
He must have understood

that first lie was certain.
Thus His penchant for anger
and all His famous acts of destruction
look a little forced, too much
like the fury we feel
when we should know better,
having lied to ourselves in secret.
But people will never learn.
Which He must have known as well.

HUSH

First rain, then sun.
First the afternoon, then acceptance.
But shouldn't there be more

to contend with,
and be comforted by?
Remember the nights

of thinking back,
telling yourself you hadn't lived
the life you wanted?

How predictable your sorrows felt.
How ordinary your few transgressions.
Who will press her cool hand

against your forehead now?
Who will sing us all a little song?
Hush, that voice might say.

As much as you've trusted
any solution, you can trust sleep.
Its long history of inspiration.

Its clear preference for justice.
How poor Macbeth was denied
its solace, and for good reason.

How you, having committed
no crime of any consequence,
will surely be received.

PERMANENCE

I can't remember how old I was,
but I used to stand in front
of the bathroom mirror, trying to imagine
what it would be like to be dead.
I thought I'd have some sense of it
if I looked far enough into my own eyes,
as if my gaze, meeting itself, would make
an absence, and exclude me.

It was an experiment, like the time
Michael Smith and I set a fire in his basement
to prove something about chemistry.
It was an idea: who I would
or wouldn't be at the end of everything,
what kind of permanence I could imagine.

In seventh grade, Michael and I
were just horsing around
when I pushed him up against that window
and we both fell through—
astonished, then afraid. Years later

his father's heart attack
could have hit at any time,
but the day it did they'd quarreled,
and before Michael walked out
to keep his fury alive, or feel sorry for himself,
he turned and yelled, I wish you were dead!

We weren't in touch. They'd moved away.
And I've forgotten who told me
the story, how ironic it was meant
to sound, or how terrible.

We could have burned down the house.
We could have been killed going through
that window. But each of us
deserves, in a reasonable life,
at least a dozen times when death
doesn't take us. At the last minute

the driver of the car coming toward us
fights off sleep and stays in his lane.
He makes it home, we make it home.
Most days are like this. You yell
at your father and later you say
you didn't mean it. And he says, I know.

You look into your own eyes in a mirror
and that's all you can see.
Until you notice the window
behind you, sunlight on the leaves
of the oak, and then the sky,
and then the clouds passing through it.

3

THE INVISIBLE

At every point
the great dazzle of the world
shines through it,

distracting you, as you should
be distracted, since all this
is life, whereas the invisible

is one of the shapes
life never chose.
Or could not hold for long.
And so, at moments,

it trembles into sight—
as the tip of a swaying branch,
or a road unwinding into the distance,

leading, perhaps, to a mountain
where you never lived
alone in a cabin, happy
to keep the fire going
on a chilly day.

And what you might have dreamt there—
has it entirely slipped away?

Moonlight makes a bed.
Arranges its thin sheets.
Now a woman is taking off her clothes.
A man is opening a door.

How pale they look—

almost transparent.

Outside, the wind stirs and rises.
A branch scrapes against the roof.
Another road unfolds into another night.

HIGH SCHOOL DAYS

The first time I saw *Rebel Without a Cause*
I knew that's what high school
was going to be like. Every new kid
had to drive an old car very fast
toward the edge of a cliff and leap out
just before it went over,
the whole crowd making chicken noises
if you saved your life too soon.
Death on the one hand, humiliation
on the other, and a few seconds in between,
after which, if you figured it right,
Natalie Wood knows who you are.
You're James Dean. You dust yourself off,
shake your head, light a cigarette.
Maybe I'd have been Sal Mineo, brainy
and nervous and needy. At the end
his gun wasn't loaded but the cops
didn't know. He was frightened
and ran toward them. *Look!* James Dean
cried out, showing them the bullets.
This didn't have to happen.
In a year he'll be dead in his car.
And since the schools in Pittsfield
were crowded and mediocre, my parents
sent me somewhere else, where I was safe
and unhappy. Even now I can feel
the allure: what I didn't want
and haven't left behind.

ENVY

Worst of them all. So many
of the other seven—lust, greed—
are only hungers, the desire for more
that moves us toward wrong action,
yet moves us.
                    But envy likes to sit alone
in a room that's almost dark, feeding
on little scraps of paper,
making excuses.
                    Since we know
pride comes before a fall, we're wary
of its pleasures, yet why not
enjoy them, we think, they seem
so forgivable.
                    But envy forgives no one,
asks no one to come closer,
hunched up and wanting
what it doesn't have.
                    Envy's made
a sullen place in the heart, envy's content
to stay there. All its language is a secret.
Until it loses even that,
becomes a habit, like ignorance,
                              but not
the blissful ignorance our parents felt
when the world was a garden, and they knew
only enough to make them yearn for more.

BIG IDEAS

I read the papers and think about hatred,
and the way ideas, especially big ideas,
look more and more like excuses for hatred.
Once hatred sets you free
you can turn to it when you need it,
but after a while, if you have a knife
or a gun, more guys on your side,
you don't need it, and you destroy the village
because you can, because it's in your way.
Every morning: more reports of suffering.
It's terrible, we say, it's awful.
But we can hear how brittle
and abstract that sounds. It's terrible
to know about it. Where is the idealism
of my youth? Where was it
even then? All around us
the war we were trying to avoid kept pressing in,
and kids like me were getting stoned and listening
to Jimi Hendrix and The Doors and then
walking off into the jungle and dying.
I don't feel guilty for refusing to fight.
I don't feel good about it either.
And I think that even then I knew too many
different things to learn to hate so purely
it could have swept me cleanly
and completely out of myself. Perhaps
that's what civilization means,
knowing too much to be able to feel
only one way. But who hasn't imagined
committing some unforgivable act?
What does it prove that most of us don't?
We watch the news, we read the papers,
afraid, sometimes, of what we understand.

THE WAY THINGS ARE IN A MOVIE

When a kid opens fire in the school cafeteria
or out on the playground or at the spring dance
nobody thinks it's real. It's when they see
their friends falling that they understand,
or maybe later, since the first one
could have stumbled, and the second
and the third might have been playing a game.

Isn't that how things are every day?
People laugh and you don't know why,
though it could be you, some note
they've scotch-taped to your back.
People fall down to show off,
and the prettiest girl's high shriek
is something she's practiced with her friends

who pretend, being beautiful, that they're not
always being watched. But you can see
who she's after, that everyone else is just
part of the crowd. It's the way things are
in a movie—if you know who's important
then you know what's going to happen
unless someone decides it has to change.

THREE EXERCISES

Begin with a cloudless sky
and wait for whatever comes next.
Little scuffles in the woods outside:
some chipmunk's great drama,
the local cat's instinctive achievement.

Shaken by the wind the leaves
look as carefully balanced
as a Calder mobile. Maybe someone
could watch them for hours.
Maybe Calder did. Or a Zen monk

who's learned not to care.
He observes the sunlight sliding
from tree to tree, and finds all this
as insignificant as the rest
of the beautiful world.

Silence next, but don't think
of the end, earth
pressing down hard, unlikely
soon to be moved. Instead,
imagine an audience

hushed and waiting,
the music about to begin,
each cough and whisper
becoming more precise, each thought
part of a pattern.

Finally, open the paper,
turn on the news:
another city in ruins.
A man dashes across the street
with a plastic jug of water.

You don't have to watch this
just because it happened.
But you'd like to care
if he dies. Snipers
in the hills are sleeping

or poised for the next clear shot.
He makes it across
or he doesn't. If he doesn't,
someone drags his body away.
Someone else takes the water home.

WHAT ANGELS FEEL VISITING HELL

Beneath the justice of it—
sorrow that there should be
so many. Then sympathy,
since that's an angel's task:

watching over
the living, reminding us
with a quick brush
of their invisible wings

to remember our better selves.
Yet all the years
of earthly failure
must dull their skill

at understanding how we feel
each time we refuse
to understand ourselves.
So an angel reports

back in heaven:
I heard the damned howling.
But what they were crying
meant nothing to me. And soon

I couldn't bear to listen.

HAMLET'S PROBLEMS

> To die, to fall asleep—
> perhaps that's all there is to it.
> —*Hamlet*, parallel text edition
> (Perfection Form Company, 1983)

No one takes him seriously when he speaks
like that, whining and moping around the castle,
getting off the occasional cruel remark,
upsetting his friends, making his mother cry—
another strung-out student who can't manage
to finish what he started. Even the ghost
has to come back to point this out.
So he kills his girlfriend's father,
but never tells her that he's sorry.
Plays hide-and-seek with the old man's body,
pretends he's crazy, pretends he's sane,
in it alone to the end. As if everything
had turned into a joke only he understands.
Even death. Especially death.
How impoverished action looks by itself—
some hopeless kid locked in his room
with his father's revolver. *That's all
there is to it*, he thinks. *So fuck it.*
At a loss to say what it might be.
Or any of the words that could make it matter.

FIGURING IT OUT

They have special effects in their bodies.
They have pictures in their bodies so they
can change into other people. But I can't
tell you what they look like. I can't
look into their bodies, because if I did
I would wake up.
      —Jennifer Raab, age 6

No one is only herself, as you discovered
when you started remembering
what happened while you slept—how quickly
anyone can change into somebody else.
And you can't look inside to find out why.

When that made you afraid
you needed to wake up,
to be back in bed and certain
everything was in its place.
There are some things we shouldn't

try to figure out—that was the message
of the movies I watched when I was growing up.
A scientist goes too far, wants to know
what's forbidden. Perhaps he needs
to bring a woman back from the dead.

Perhaps he takes a heart and a brain
and puts them together.
Shrewd and brilliant, he conceals his madness
from the world, even from himself.
But I wasn't interested in believing

I'd be punished if I crossed some line.
I wanted to see the monster run amok.
The peasants kept taunting him,
and running amok was in his nature.
At the end his creator has to admit

the error you understood when you were six.
And then the monster has to die,
although someone's always waiting
to make the same mistake—rebuild the lab,
stitch the pieces back together—

someone who won't stop at death,
who claims there's nothing he shouldn't know.

MEANINGFUL THINGS

> There's a peculiar mechanism in
> writers' minds. They don't really want
> to accept that the things that they find
> meaningful and build into their works
> are going to become outdated, arcane
> and finally obscure.
> > —Professor Robert L. Oakman,
> > creator of Medialink,
> > a computer program for attaching
> > multimedia material to a printed text

Times change, and we forget.
A writer puts his hero in a Packard.
Kids today can't see it.
So you hit a key and there's the car,
then the building he'd have parked
in front of, then the bar in that building
where the next scene takes place.

So many meaningful things get lost.
Isn't it natural to resist?
Here in New Hampshire, thinking
about what to write, I'm only certain
I can't make fun of Professor Oakman,
who's obviously trying to help.
And I'm wondering

if Lance at Valley Automotive
will have my Honda fixed by four.
The brakes just feel a little loose,
I told him. And there's some sort
of puffing sound when you press the pedal.
I could see Lance was used to this kind
of imprecision. I'll take a look
at the calipers, he said.

Great writers find
their annotators, serious readers
turn to the notes. The rest of us
make the necessary leap: he drives
his black Packard from her house to the bar
on Central Avenue. He's thinking
she's the kind of blonde who's so languid
and shadowy she speaks out of nowhere.
You can't lay a finger on her,
he tells himself. You shouldn't even try.

MY LIFE BEFORE I KNEW IT

I liked rainy days
when you didn't have to go outside and play.
At night I'd tell my sister
there were snakes under her bed.
When I mowed the lawn I imagined being famous.
Cautious and stubborn, unwilling to fail,
I knew for certain what I didn't want to know.

I hated to dance. I hated baseball,
and collected airplane cards instead.
I learned to laugh at jokes I didn't get.
The death of Christ moved me,
but only at the end of *Ben-Hur*.
I thought Henry Mancini was a great composer.

My secret desire was to own a collie
who would walk with me in the woods
when the leaves were falling
and I was thinking about writing the stories
that would make me famous.

Sullen, overweight, melancholy,
writers didn't have to be good at sports.
They stayed inside for long periods of time.
They often wore glasses. But strangers
were moved by what they accomplished
and wrote them letters. One day

one of those strangers would introduce
herself to me, and then
the life I'd never been able to foresee
would begin, and everything
before I became myself would appear
necessary to the rest of the story.

FRAGILE

Sometimes the world insists
that we think about our places in it—
how fragile they feel, each one
nudging the next. So many inscriptions
already written. Here lies.
Beloved of. Remembered forever.

Fragile: shattery, shivery, gone.

When you're old enough to have felt
(alone, at night)
the kind of pain a few pills
won't take care of,
then maybe you've wondered—

If I died now, what would I leave behind
that would hurt me, what secrets
that would change the minds
of those who loved me?

Think of the man with his hidden shelves
of pornography. He knew he was dying.
He left it that way. He didn't ask:
When shall I destroy all of this?
Who shall I turn myself into?

Brittle, delicate, severable.

Like a leg, or an arm, any part
we can lose without losing ourselves.
Like an exquisite object whose beauty
is blended with the fact
that it isn't meant to last.

All afternoon the sky is full
of enormous clouds, ominous,
mutable. Yet the rain holds off.
We go out to play tennis,
return to eat dinner.

Whatever allows us to be here
thinking as well as we can
we're ready to praise.

4

FALSE NOCTURNE

Learning how to play the piano, I favored
the most melancholy pieces
because they were slow,
and my hesitations blurred
into the semblance of feeling.

In the music we listened to at school
we heard donkeys descending
into the canyon, followed by a storm.
As if the point of art
was to make us think of something else.

Anxious to step outside
my parents' lives, I was unwilling
to give up anything I actually owned.
Tacked to my desk:
a picture of a monk

ringing a bell in his garden
on a cloudy autumn morning.
At twenty I was determined
to be unhappy, or to sound that way.
But what do I know now

about that moody young man?
How easy to make him look foolish,
who taught me, even then,
how I'd learn to change my mind.
Who kept in his notebook

the story of the piano student
who asked her teacher,
Should I play in time, or in accordance
with my feelings? And he replied,
Why not try to feel in time?

EMILY DICKINSON'S HOUSE

"It is true," Emily Dickinson wrote
one day, looking out
of her window, "that the unknown
is the largest need of intellect,
although for this no one thinks
to thank God." Almost all my life
I've lived not far away,
but I've never been to her house.
I don't know if her desk
is near a window,
or what she might have seen
through the wavy glass: trees, sky,
another house, the familiar
facts of the world
which she knew must be resisted.
Or learned so well
their strangeness is restored
each time we look: maple and elm,
clouds or sun, then rain,
the neighbor's house (a man inside
reading a book), and then
the unseen moor, and the narrow wind
that sweeps across it.

REASONS

Some people hear God speaking
inside their heads, others
from a shrub or a dog.
God tells a man it's time
to kill his wife and children.
He has to do it. Or God says,
Whores shouldn't be allowed to live—
pick any one of them on the street.
But sometimes God chooses not to explain.
Saints and heroes make the most
of their visions, and in this
art helps (all those grand
and gruesome paintings), but success
is what finally matters—a nation saved,
faith preserved, history writing down
their stories. Without that,
the man who'd been told to slay his enemies
ends up in a locked room
swaying from side to side all day
with his arms strapped behind his back.
The world is designed to accommodate this.
The idea of God is designed
to accommodate this—the transcendent
over here, the cursed down there.
And so for some (the faithful,
the lucky) life
adds up, and on their death-beds
a beckoning light appears
to comfort them. But for others
(a defective gene, no more than that)
memory is stripped away so slowly
they keep forgetting if they ever believed
there must be a reason for such cruelty.

ABROAD

> People do not die immediately for us,
> but remain bathed in a sort of aura of
> life . . . It is as though they were
> traveling abroad.
>
> —Marcel Proust

His plans were always changing—

a few more weeks in Rome,
another month in the country
since the fine weather
promised to continue.

How often he thought of you
waiting at home.
Of course he was eager to return.
Yet life was different now.
It was hard to explain.

And when you were certain
you'd received the last of his letters,
you were finally able
to feel abandoned.

You walked along the beach
thinking of the ocean's great weight,
kicking at a stone in the sand,
letting the wind lift your hair.

How far the wind had come to touch you!

Your heart trembled to imagine
such distances—the wildness of the sea,
and the shores beyond,

where a man would shake his head
if you asked for help,

or gesture with his hands
to say, But I cannot help you.
I do not know what you want.
I do not understand
why you have come here.

THE NIGHT SKY

In the book you've been reading
it's the end of the season.
The shades have been drawn
in that house by the lake,

and a woman is standing
alone on the porch. She thinks,
There's no sense pretending
I could have been happy here.

A few notes from a piano
float across the water,
and you wonder if that isn't
more than is needed—

how the music suggests
the idea of change
gathering in the distance.
But not for her. She'll return

to her father, who drinks too much,
having failed as a doctor, then
as a farmer. She can see
him asleep in his chair

after dinner, a small fire
in the grate, snow in the garden.
And on the table, the bills
to be paid. He'd be lost

in bitterness without her,
which she understands. So this
is a story about accommodation,
how quiet feelings come to matter

and finally suffice.
She watches the wind fall back
across the water. And you think:
But she deserves to be happy.

Perhaps, in the final few pages,
something unexpected will occur.
Perhaps only the moon will rise.
Yet her life is this book

and when the moon appears
at last in the night sky
that may be all the story requires.
Now her thoughts are as real

for you as they must be
for her, the way it was
when you first fell in love.
You could be standing beside her.

She could be waiting
to be touched. But why
is he waiting, she wonders,
if he knows how I feel?

THE QUESTIONS POEMS ASK

Watching a couple of crows
playing around in the woods, swooping
in low after each other, I wonder
if they ever slam into the trees.

There's an answer here, unlike
most questions in poems,
which are left up in the air.
Was it a vision or a waking dream?

You decide, says the poet.
You do some of this work,
but think carefully.
Some people want to believe

poetry is anything
they happen to feel. That way
they're never wrong. Others yearn
for the difficult:

insoluble problems, secret codes
not meant to be broken.
Nobody, they've discovered,
ever means what he says.

But rarely does a crow
hit a tree, though other, clumsier birds
bang into them all the time, and we say
these birds have not adapted well

to the forest environment.
Frequently stunned, they become
easy prey for the wily fox,
who's learned how to listen

for that snapping of branches
and collapsing of wings,
who knows where to go
and what to do when he gets there.

THE POLE

We were back at college, young again.
She was someone I yearned for
throughout the spring
of my senior year. In the dream
it was evening and she was having dinner
with her friends when I appeared
at the door and waved to her
until she came out onto the porch where I
was standing with a long wooden pole,
maybe five or six feet high. I said
I had brought it to her because
I'd heard she was going rock climbing.
Yes, she said, but you don't need
poles to go rock climbing. Which I knew.
From the beginning of the dream I'd been aware
that was the case. Which meant
nothing would happen between us,
although the strangeness of my gesture
didn't seem to trouble her. She smiled at me.
And in the dream I remembered where
the pole had come from. I could see it
leaning against the wall beside the blackboard
of my third or fourth grade classroom,
a long pole with a metal hook on top
used to lower the shades that covered
that room's many tall and empty windows.

THE LUMINISTS

The light of the moment becoming a memory—
that was their subject: as if the present
could be haunted by its own nostalgia.
Or perhaps that wasn't exactly the subject.
And a desolate sweep of beach reflects
only an afternoon when no one was there.

All of these places look emptier
than they were: unmarked,
unfulfilled, atremble. "Spirit of repose,"
"silent energy of nature"—that's the way
you could think if you believed
the landscape was more than a mirror.

Yet even de Tocqueville had to imagine
he might be one of the last travelers.
So the beautiful solitudes of America
were "touching," their pleasures "melancholy."
One felt "in some sort of hurry to admire them."

That he himself was there was only one of the signs.

MY SPIRITUAL LIFE

Nothing mysterious ever happened
in our church. Those suspicious transformations,
wine into blood, spirit into flesh,
were comfortably symbolic. Scrubbed clean,
our windows let in the cold New England light.
White clapboards, white walls, a cross
without Jesus, an altar like a lectern.
The year my father was deacon, my mother
sliced the squares of bread for communion.
She said it did nothing for her.
She disliked being told she was a sinner,
resented the assumption that she needed
to be forgiven. Sin was for the Catholics,
she said, and the Episcopalians, who might as well
be Catholics, except they were richer
and had to have a more impressive church.
I never took Sunday School seriously
after I learned we wouldn't be graded.
Something like that would happen eventually,
but then, being dead, we'd understand
what now we couldn't possibly understand.
So it was foolish, my mother thought,
to worry too much about heaven,
especially if so many were going to be excluded,
having chosen one of the wrong religions.
Faith looked a lot like believing
you were right, or your parents had been.
The sun slammed in through those tall, clear windows.
Our minister explained that we were good,
but could be better. Think about it,
turn it over in our hearts. Finally God would decide.
Week by week we were on our own.

THE BEST DAYS

for Judy and Jenny

It's hard to be happy, harder still
to talk about it. Walking together
through these intimate woods, the coins
of light scattered all around us,
it's enough to praise the weather. No need
to disentangle what we feel
from what we think. Or even
to acknowledge the world, not far away,
assembling its important troubles.
The best days, like this one, float
at the borders of our lives, as unremarkable
as light, or the fluttering of leaves.
We know we can't live here.
Perhaps the hermit, having turned his back
on us all, thinks he lives here.
Or the saint, forever trusting
in another life. But we don't envy them.
At evening they must sit down alone
to bless their hunger,
which, perhaps, also makes them happy,
then uneasy, as if they had betrayed
some hard allegiance
to feel this way, the way we feel.

MY LIFE AT THE MOVIES

Village of the Damned was the movie I'd chosen
for my first date with Emily, my first
date ever, as well as my last with Emily.
It was a good movie—children with supernatural powers
turn against their parents and take over the village.
But I kept remembering how embarrassed I'd felt
telling Emily on the phone that we'd be going
to a horror movie. Science fiction, I thought
immediately. God, that sounds so much better.

Then there was *The Wreck of the Mary Deare*
with Barbara, who showed up late, so we missed
the credits and the opening scene, and never
went out again. Later *Hour of the Wolf* with Wendy
and Max von Sydow as a demented artist
who must stay awake all night to fend off his demons.

These were not, I can see now, the very best choices.
Certainly they failed to create a comfortable
romantic mood. At least with *Blow-Up*, Nancy and I
had the mystery of the end to talk about.
What does it mean when the photographer
walks away and vanishes, like the body
he'd discovered in the park? That was the Sixties,
a good time to discuss illusion and reality,
an easy time to favor illusion. When we got stoned

and watched *A Night at the Opera* it was amazing
to see how much was going on. Groucho,
we agreed, was a genius, like James Joyce,
in fact very much like James Joyce.
Our teachers were resistant, failing to grasp
the necessary connections. Was Stephen Dedalus
like all four Marx Brothers, or only Groucho?
It was so difficult to explain. We cited

Baudelaire, mentioned the limitations
of rational thought, and were given extensions.

Movies, of course, were much better
than rational thought. Plus they had music.
How could I drive off down the highway without
the right song in my mind? How could I
break up with Nancy without seeing it played out
on the screen: a crane shot, lifting me up
and back and away in one long sweet and floating glide.
Then a slow dissolve. Or the final frame
frozen into significance. Of course

it didn't happen that way, and now
I don't remember the truth. Instead
I think of the last scene of *La Dolce Vita*—
Mastroianni on the beach, so handsome
and anguished. A young girl at the water's edge
calls to him, but he can't hear what she's saying.
Then he smiles and shrugs
as only he could shrug, as if to say he knew

that whatever lost part of his life
she represented, it was too far away from him now.
Knowing that, he could only smile
and shrug, which meant: What can I do?
We can't take the world
too seriously, no matter how lovely
you are in your white dress this morning.

VANISHING

First you worry that you'll never get
what you want, later that you'll lose
what you have. In between
for a time you just trusted
the course of your life, assumed
things would fall into place.
Most of them did. But now,
not quite all of a sudden, every new pain
is a sign, then a promise.
Even if you didn't take death seriously
when you were young, you understood
that was the story. Your kids
leave home, your dog sleeps most of the day.
Letters arrive wanting to know
if you've planned for the future.
You walk out on the porch:
there's a field, then a mountain,
so familiar you have to look hard.
The letters say, It's never too late.
All things vanish. You know that.
All the things you love
vanish. Can you love this idea?
Is that the task? you think. To try?

ABOUT THE AUTHOR

Lawrence Raab was born in Pittsfield, Massachusetts, in 1946. He received a B.A. from Middlebury College and an M.A. from Syracuse University. He has received the Bess Hokin Award from *Poetry*, a Junior Fellowship from the University of Michigan Society of Fellows, and grants from the National Endowment for the Arts and the Massachusetts Council on the Arts. His poems have appeared in numerous magazines, including *Poetry*, *The New Yorker*, *The Paris Review*, *The Kenyon Review*, *The Nation*, and *Salmagundi*. He is the author of four previous collections of poems, *Mysteries of the Horizon* (Doubleday, 1972), *The Collector of Cold Weather* (The Ecco Press, 1976), *Other Children* (Carnegie-Mellon University Press, 1987), and *What We Don't Know About Each Other* (Penguin, 1993), as well as a chapbook of collaborative poems with Stephen Dunn, *Winter at the Caspian Sea* (Palanquin Press, 1999). His poems have been included in several anthologies, including *The Best American Poetry 1992* and *1993*, and *A Book of Luminous Things*. He is professor of English at Williams College in Williamstown, Massachusetts, where he has taught since 1976. *What We Don't Know About Each Other* was chosen as a National Book Award finalist.

PENGUIN POETS